Michael Grinder

ONE MAN'S JOURNEY

the search for self

Illustrated by Inez Lawson

CELESTIAL ARTS

MILLBRAE, CALIFORNA

Copyright©1975 by Celestial Arts
231 Adrian Road, Millbrae, California 94030

No part of this book may be reproduced by
any mechanical, photographic, or electronic
process, or in the form of a phonographic
recording, nor may it be stored in a retrieval
system, transmitted, or otherwise copied for
public or private use without the written
permission of the publisher.

First Printing, May 1975
Made in the United States of America

Library of Congress Cataloging in Publication Data

Grinder, Michael.
   One man's journey.

   Poems.
   I. Title.
PS3557.R52505   811'.5'4   74-25840
ISBN 0-89087-013-6

ONE MAN'S JOURNEY

May the Sun
     of the bright moments
     of your relationship
Shine
     so that
you may bask
     in the
intensity of love.

&

May the Moon
     of the dark moments
     of your relationship
peek through enough
     so that
negative emotions
     are seen as
positive feelings frustrated.

Love
is a relationship,
Love
is not a feeling.
time
is the variable which differentiates
love   from   fascination.

*I especially love my relationship
with Mary when I am at the point
where when Mary receives pleasure,
I do also.*

I love that   part of me
that I experience   when
I think of you . . .   and
thereby love you and me together.

My capacity to love
            lies more in myself
than the person I am loving . . .
I cannot give
            what I don't
already have for myself.

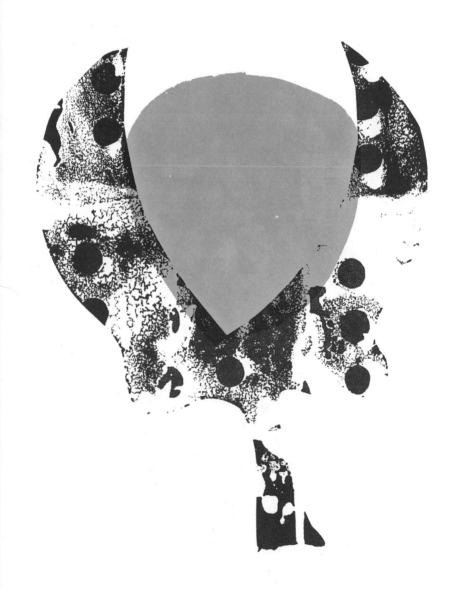

I have such a need to express myself
that sometimes when I say, "I love you"
please don't reply.
I want to experience giving without
feeling like I am giving to receive.

I am able to free myself according to the amount that I don't bind myself to expectations that I formed in the past.

When Krista wants attention. . .
my daughter behaves so that she elicits
a response from me.
Whether she receives
            a
negative   or   positive
            feedback
depends on how soon I give her
            my attention.

When
       you say to me,
       "I love you," I respond
because not to respond
is too overwhelming. . .
I am just now learning
to feel worthy enough to
listen to a compliment in silence.

When I feel that
Mary is excited
not just to be receiving
but excited
because she is receiving
from me. . .

> *I feel more*
> *powerful and*
> *want to give*
> *m o r e.*

*The mystery of life
is found in the
celebration of it.*

The most I can do is avail myself of love.
The free choosing to commit oneself to
another is the richness of love. . .
one's ability to realize that the commitment
is to the now allows one to enjoy the
pleasures of that richness.

*I can love another only
as much   as   I love myself.*

WHEN I LOVE

WHEN I HATE

WHEN I LOVE

WHEN I HATE

WHEN I HATE

WHEN I LOVE

I have a hard time accepting myself
                              when I hate.
. . .and an easy time   *when I love.*
Yet I know that my capacity   *to hate &*
                              to love
                              are the same,
for they come from the same source.
Which means that when I don't accept my
                              negative feelings
                    I deaden positive feelings
                              as well.

My mental health is measured
by
HOW much I am in the now.

FAMILY LOVE

Love is diffusive
expanding and bonding with another
until life becomes its own reward.

Love is diffusive
even unto itself.

Love becomes pure
as the giver finds
oneself in the giving.

Love is diffusive
even unto itself
renewing and refreshing itself.

Love grows and begets yet others
and in so doing enlarges
itself to include
their sorrow as well as their joy.

Love is diffusive
even unto itself
renewing and refreshing itself
finding meaning in itself.

Love which formerly was
embedded in possessing, matures
and takes the form of parting
with the begotten ones
as they become
selves unto themselves.

Love is diffusive
even unto itself
renewing and refreshing itself
finding meaning in itself
finding meaning in itself.

I have two levels of freedom:
"freedom from"
&
"freedom toward."

The first type is one in which my efforts
are to remove myself from conditions of
obligations & responsibilities.
Whereas the second freedom is a desire
to expand and enlarge myself in new areas.

Peace can be as open
and as often,
and as meaningful
as you wish to make it.

Peace can be a way of life
or it can be an occasional happening,
but anyway you know it
or use it
it still has its special message and meaning.

Tony C.

When I withhold the full force
of the emotions that I am feeling
it is
    because I am afraid that the
                        other
will expect me to be that way
          all the time.
I am really comfortable with people
                     who
accept me for HOW I am at the time.
I am freed to experience myself
               more fully.

I used to perceive
"how I felt"   *was all important*
now
"whether I can accept myself" *is.*

*The THINK pattern of a life style
is "I should. . . ."
The FEEL pattern of a life style
is "I feel. . . ."*

The ultimate for me
                          is
                          to
                                form an inner core
a friend. . .
                   my friend would
                              give
                                   permission
to all the rest of me to be however I am.

Part of my maturity is
s u f f e r i n g
from my immaturity.

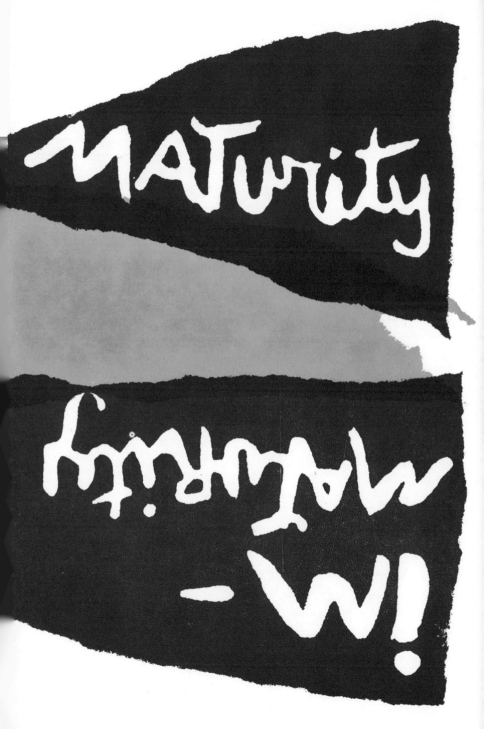

I am in a conversation
and talk
in generalities
leaving. . .
I feel incomplete—
I didn't expose my
vulnerable,
personal,
self.

When I think
          of my relationships
          with others
I often ask
          "How am I?"
          "How do I feel?"
When I ask
          "How accepting am I?"
I find much more of myself.

Grief that is shared
is borne in hope.

Sometimes I can sense a situation better than I can think out the situation . . . If I limit myself to that which I can verify . . . my perceptions would be severely limited.

I listen best
when I hear and allow ambivalences
and don't impose myself on the other
in the form of judgments.

When I say that I can talk to someone
I mean that he not only answers and
responds to my statements
    but he also says how he is reacting to me.

*When I keep replaying the past
events it is because I didn't
get myself out — I didn't
voice my gut.
I really am mad at myself
with these "left-overs." I
keep myself from involvement
in the NOW.*

*"Shoulds" are expectations
that I have allowed others
to assign to me.*

A friend
      is someone
            who doesn't
A friend   *have to answer my needs.*
      is someone
             who listens. . .
             so that having needs is OK.

My friends are pillars which support me through
s p a n s
o f
over-risks.

*My life style is appropriate
when I am able to be in "riskful situations"
without "over-risking" — getting lost.*

*I would rather be disliked
for what I am
than to be liked for what
I am not.*

　　　　　　　Rene

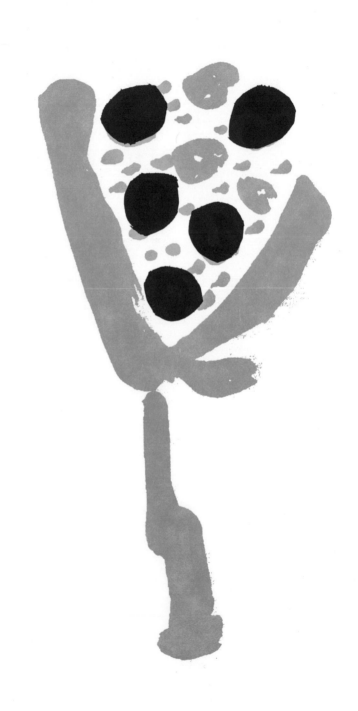

My maturity is seen,
not so much in the absence of problems,
as   in my coping with them.

The irony of me being dead is that I don't realize that I am. . .only with awareness do I have a choice as to how alive I want to be.

*It is much easier for me to see reality
distorted in either extremes.
Reality is complex. . .I am neither the
greatest   nor   the worst.*

To grow old and remain new and alive inside
is

to add depth   *instead of years*
to   *to*
JOY   *AGE.*

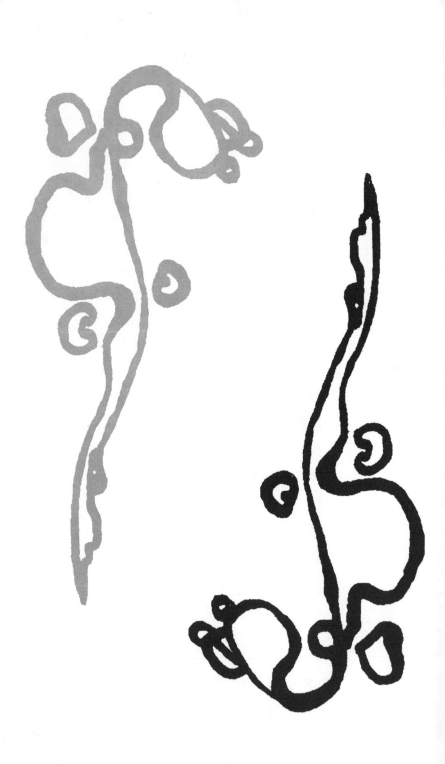

Sometimes
> *I need a relationship*
> *in which I am fulfilled*
> *because I'm accepted.*

And at other times
> *I need a relationship*
> *in which I am fulfilled*
> *because I'm challenged.*

I guess it depends on how secure
I am feeling about myself.

The BASIS of conversing in a relationship is
the ABILITY of each person to be the other
and listen without judging.
The KEY to conversing is to KNOW when one can be the
other and when one cannot.
The SUCCESS of conversing is only TRYING to be the other
when one can.

*The distance between
my words   &   my awareness
of an interaction is the amount that
I have deadened myself.*

Oh, I know I give compliments;
they may be given out of compulsion. . .
in which case, I need you to hear them
in a certain way
*   or*
they may be voluntary. . .
in which case I am OK
with however you receive them.

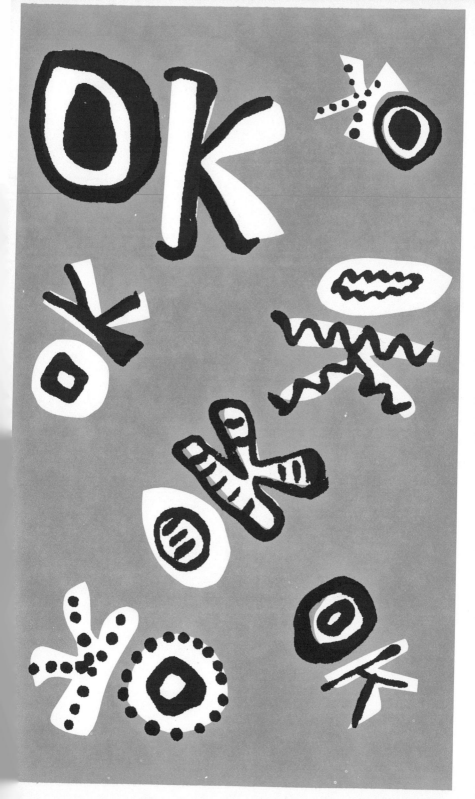

I want to be
enough of a friend   to share
&
enough of a brother   not to impose.

The tragedy of my "I should. . ."
is that beneath it is an
"I want. . ."
which I don't experience.

While it is true that
anxiety is the result of
having expectations. . .
it is even truer that
having anxiety is the result of
having an inability
to change expectations.

Love never has to be qualified.
Others cannot earn my love, nor
can I merit theirs. Love cannot
be possessed or taken for granted.
Love has an existence apart from
the wishes and desires of those
who have or seek it.

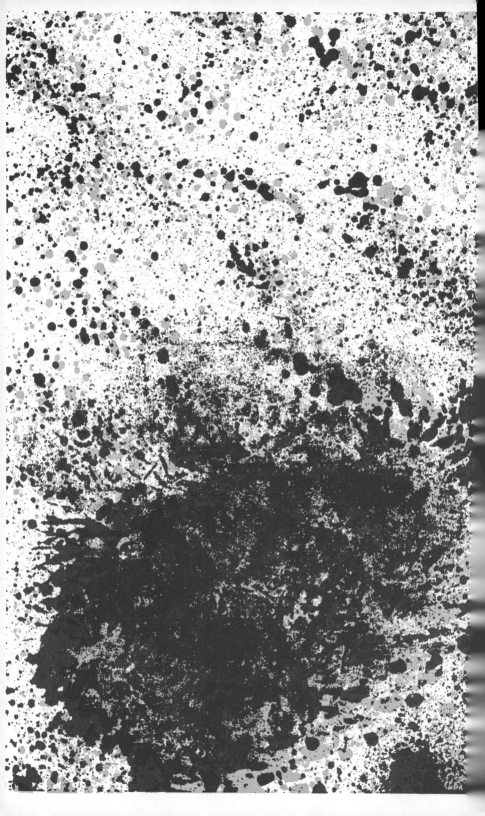

A healthy relationship is formed when one links up with another without forming knots.

*The secret of affection
is   to   make
every tenderness last
as   long   as   possible.*

*The presence or absences of inner conflict
doesn't determine if I feel free or not. . .
It's whether I am accepting of them or not.*

ITIMACY
is the exposing
owning & sharing
one's emotional needs with another.

What I treasure of our love is
that no one will know but we two;
and what I thrill at is that "knowing"
is not "knowing" but "living."

What I like best about you
(and us)
is that I don't know what
I like best about you
(and us).

My life with Mary
is a relationship
of trying
      not to let
past "impressions and images
of what our relationship
would be like"
interfere
      with how we are
in the here and now.

Being "open-minded"
is
being able to change expectations.

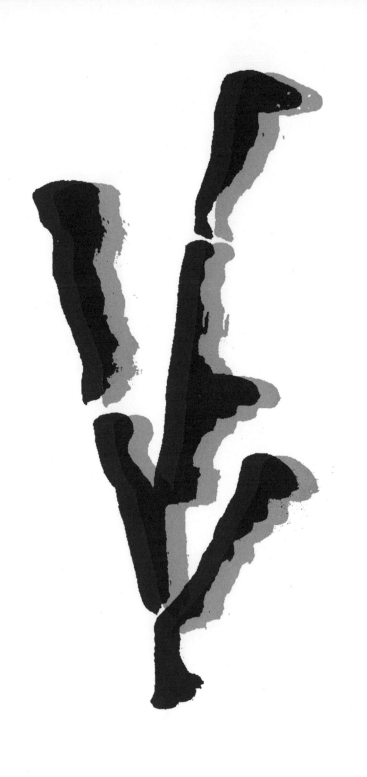

A vacation is an occasion to slow down incoming experiences so that past unfinished experiences can be given their needed attention.

If then, at the end of my life,
they would ask me,
*   "If you were to do it all over again*
*   would you live it differently?"*
and I thought of that part I shared with you
I would answer a grateful "NO."

CELESTIAL ARTS BOOK LIST

LOVE IS AN ATTITUDE, poetry and photographs by Walter Rinder.
03-0 Paper @ $3.95   04-9 Cloth @ $7.95

THIS TIME CALLED LIFE, poetry and photographs by Walter Rinder.
05-7 Paper @ $3.95   06-5 Cloth @ $7.95

SPECTRUM OF LOVE, poetry by Walter Rinder with David Mitchell art.
19-7 Paper @ $2.95   20-0 Cloth @ $7.95

FOLLOW YOUR HEART, poetry by Walter Rinder with Richard Davis art.
39-1 Paper @ $2.95

THE HUMANNESS OF YOU, Vol. 1, art and philosophy by Walter Rinder.
47-2 Paper @ $2.95

THE HUMANNESS OF YOU, Vol. 2, art and philosophy by Walter Rinder.
54-5 Paper @ $2.95

VISIONS OF YOU, poetry by George Betts and photography by Robert Scales.
07-3 Paper @ $3.95

MY GIFT TO YOU, poetry by George Betts and photography by Robert Scales.
15-4 Paper @ $3.95

YOU & I, poetry and photography by Leonard Nimoy.
26-X Paper @ $3.95   27-8 Cloth @ $7.95

WILL I THINK OF YOU?, poetry and photography by Leonard Nimoy.
70-7 Paper @ $3.95

SPEAK THEN OF LOVE, poetry by Andrew Oerke with Asian art.
29-4 Paper @ $3.95

I AM, concepts of awareness in poetic form by Michael Grinder with color art.
25-1 Paper @ $2.95

GAMES STUDENTS PLAY, transactional analysis in schools by Ken Ernst.
16-2 Paper @ $3.95   17-0 Cloth @ $7.95

GUIDE FOR SINGLE PARENTS, transactional analysis by Kathryn Hallett.
55-3 Paper @ $3.95   64-2 Cloth @ $7.95

PASSIONATE MIND, guidance and understanding by Joel Kramer.
63-4 Paper @ $3.95

SENSIBLE BOOK, understanding children's senses by Barbara Polland.
53-7 Paper @ $3.95

THIS TIMELESS MOMENT, Aldous Huxley's life by Laura Huxley.
22-5 Paper @ $4.95

HEALING MIND, explains the healing powers of the mind by Dr. Irving Oyle.
80-4 Paper @ $4.95

HOW TO BE SOMEBODY, a guide for personal growth by Yetta Bernhard.
20-9 Paper @ $4.95

CREATIVE SURVIVAL, the problems of single mothers by Persia Woolley.
17-9 Paper @ $4.95

FAT LIBERATION, the awareness technique to losing weight by Alan Dolit.
03-9 Paper @ $3.95

ALPHA BRAIN WAVES, explanation of same by D. Boxerman and A. Spilken.
16-0 Paper @ $4.95

INWARD JOURNEY, art as therapy by Margaret Keyes.
81-2 Paper @ $4.95

GOD, poetic visions of the abstract by Alan Watts.
75-8 Paper @ $3.95

Write for a free catalog to:
CELESTIAL ARTS   231 Adrian Road   Millbrae, California 94030